A World of Food

FRANCE

Kathy Elgin

CLARA
HOUSE
BOOKS

Minneapolis

First published in 2010 by Clara House Books, an imprint of The Oliver Press, Inc.

Clara House Books
5707 West 36th Street
Minneapolis, MN 55416
USA

Produced by Arcturus Publishing Limited

The right of Kathy Elgin to be identified as the author of this work has been asserted by her in accordance with the Copyright, Designs and Patents Act 1988.

Series concept: Alex Woolf
Editor: Alex Woolf
Designer: Jane Hawkins
Map illustrator: Stefan Chabluk
Picture researcher: Alex Woolf

Picture Credits
Art Archive: 7 (Gianni Dagli Orti).
Bridgeman Art Library: 6.
Corbis: 4 (Steven Vidler/Eurasia Press), 10 (Michael Boys), 13 (Stefano Amantini/Atlantide Phototravel), 14 (Owen Franken), 15 (Franck Guiziou/Hemis), 16 (Clay McLachlan/Aurora Photos), 17 (Owen Franken), 18 (Bernard Annebicque/Sygma), 19 (Dung Vo Trung/Sygma), 22 (Owen Franken), 23 (Owen Franken), 24 (H Amiard/PhotoCuisine), 25 *crepe* (Riou/PhotoCuisine), 26 (Owen Franken), 28 (Floris Leeuwenberg/The Cover Story), 29 (Andreas Gebert/dpa).
Getty Images: cover and 20 (Jack Guez/AFP).
Shutterstock: 8 (Elena Elisseeva), 9 (Andreas G Karelias), 11 (Andreas G Karelias), 12 (Tomo Jesenicnik), 21 *beaten egg* (Peter Baxter), 21 *sugar* (Juris Sturainis), 21 *almond flour* (Olga Lyubkina), 21 *Galette des Rois* (Madeleine Openshaw), 25 *sifted flour* (Clive Watkins), 25 *red mixing bowl* (Thomas M Perkins), 25 *butter* (Tomasz Trojanowski), 27 *eggplant, onions, zucchini* (Sandra Caldwell), 27 *red pepper* (Serp), 27 *green pepper* (Iakov Kalinin), 27 *olive oil, basil* (yamix), 27 *ratatouille* (Monkey Business Images).

Every attempt has been made to clear copyright. Should there be any inadvertent omission, please apply to the publisher for rectification.

Library of Congress Cataloging-in-Publication Data

Elgin, Kathy.
France / Kathy Elgin.
        p. cm. -- (A world of food)
Includes bibliographical references and index.
ISBN 978-1-934545-10-2
1. Food habits--France--Juvenile literature. 2. Cookery, French--Juvenile literature. 3. France--Social life and customs--Juvenile literature. I. Title. II. Series.

GT2853.F7E44 2010
394.1'20944--dc22

                                              2009041342

Dewey Decimal Classification Number: 394.1'2'0944

ISBN 978-1-934545-10-2

Printed in China

www.oliverpress.com

Contents

La Belle France!

France is a large country on the western edge of Europe. It has 22 separate regions, each divided into several "departments."

The people in each region are very proud of their individual identity. They like to express this by keeping up the old traditions. They wear regional costumes on special occasions and eat dishes made from local products. Because of this, it's hard to find just one style of cooking that is typically French.

Fresh food

Whatever part of the country they live in, the French love food. They are used to fresh meat, fish, and vegetables, good wine and a varied diet.

In the past, most French people were farmers. They grew their own crops and kept a few animals. These days they

L'ILE DE FRANCE

CAFÉ TABAC L'ILE DE FRANCE TAB

▶ A sidewalk cafe is the perfect place to meet friends, relax after sightseeing, or just sit and watch the world go by.

can afford to buy imported food and eat in foreign restaurants, but they still prefer local food made from fresh ingredients. They also like to eat whatever food is in season at that time of year.

Tradition

In country regions, people cook traditional recipes handed down from one generation to another. Many people in rural France eat food similar to what their ancestors ate.

In cities, by contrast, food on the menu in a restaurant often involves complicated recipes. These include meat cooked in a rich sauce with wine or with butter and cream. This is known as haute cuisine, or "top-quality cooking."

The French talk about food a lot. They even argue about it! Wherever you go in France, you are sure of a good meal.

▲ This map of France shows the locations of some of the places mentioned in this book.

FRENCH FOOD AND DRINK

Word	Pronunciation	Meaning
baguette	ba-get	long, thin bread
boeuf	be(r)f	beef
café au lait	ka-fay oh lay	coffee with milk
croissant	krwa-son	a sweet, flaky, crescent-shaped pastry
fromage	fraw-maj	cheese
jambon	zham-bohn	ham
pain	pen	bread
pâtisserie	pa-tee-seree	cake shop

Ancient Roots

France was originally part of the Roman Empire. The Romans introduced many new crops, including grain for bread making, a variety of vegetables, and olives for oil. They also grew grapes for making wine. This became very important in France.

Medieval meals

In the Middle Ages, most people ate whatever was available in their region each season. The rich, however, had lavish banquets with lots of dishes served all together. Thick, spicy sauces were used to make dried or preserved food taste better.

Things changed in 1533, when the Italian princess Catherine de' Medici came to France to marry the future King Henry II. She brought Italian cooks with her, and a more sophisticated way of eating.

▲ This painting shows a feast being served in the dining hall of a medieval castle. In the top right-hand corner, musicians are playing in the minstrels' gallery.

Celebrity chefs

In the 18th century, cooks at the royal court began to write down their recipes. From then on, French food became famous all over Europe, and so did the chefs.

One of the most famous chefs was Marie-Antoine Carême. He was famous for his spectacular desserts. They looked like fantastic buildings made of marzipan, pastry, and sugar. His main dishes, however, were still based on rich sauces and took a long time to cook.

Keeping it simple

In the 19th century, Auguste Escoffier made recipes more simple. He used healthier sauces made with vegetables instead of cream and butter. He also served one course at a time, instead of all the dishes together.

In Escoffier's kitchen, all of the chefs had separate jobs, so they became skilled at making sauces, roasting meat, or making pastry. This made cooking and serving much quicker. It was a revolution!

▼ This is a reconstruction of the kitchen of a French chateau from the early 1900s. The pink dessert near the man with the chef's hat is just like one of Carême's impressive "architectural" puddings.

Looking at France

France is shaped like a hexagon. Three of its sides are bordered by the sea. The other three form land borders with other countries.

The French landscape ranges from flat plains to snow-capped mountains and hot, sandy beaches. The climate, too, differs from one region to another.

▲ Bright yellow sunflowers and purple lavender make the fields of Provence a spectacular sight in summer.

The north

In the north and west the land is flat, with gentle hills and plains. The soil here is fertile, and good for growing grain crops. Flat land is also good for building on, and today there is a lot of industry here. Paris, the capital of France, is in this area. The climate here is cool and often windy.

The south

The center and south are dominated by high mountain ranges. In the far south, the Pyrenees mark the border with Spain. In the southeast, France is separated from Italy and Switzerland by the Alps. The mountains are covered in snow all winter, and people go there to ski.

In the center of France there is another mountainous region called the Massif Central. This is a very ancient volcanic area, with thickly wooded valleys, flat plateaus, rivers, and lakes.

By the sea

France has hundreds of miles of coastline, which means lots of fresh fish. On the west is the Atlantic Ocean. The coast here is very rugged, with high cliffs and few beaches. The climate is mild and wet, with winter storms.

The Mediterranean coast in the southeast is much flatter. There are sandy beaches and small fishing villages. The climate here features hot, sunny summers and mild winters.

▶ The rugged coast of Brittany is beautiful but can be dangerous when winter storms are blowing.

HIDDEN FRANCE

The terrain of the Massif Central makes communications and travel very difficult. In the past, the area and its people were cut off from the rest of the country. They still feel different from other French people.

Working the Land

Agriculture has always been part of French life. Many families have their own small farm. They keep a few cattle, sheep, or pigs, and grow fruit and vegetables. They often sell produce from the farm gate.

Corn and cattle

The flat land of the north is just right for growing corn, wheat, oats, and barley. Dairy cattle are also kept here, and their milk is made into cheese.

The best cattle for meat are the Charolais, bred in Burgundy in the southeast. One of the famous dishes of the region, Beef Burgundy, is beef cooked in local red wine.

The Garden of France

The Loire region is known as the "Garden of France." It has orchards full of apples, pears, peaches, and cherries. Fruit tarts are the local specialty.

In the south, the Mediterranean climate makes it possible to grow citrus fruits such as oranges and lemons, as well as olives and peppers.

▶ In the gardens of the chateau of Villandry, in the Loire, flowers and vegetables grow together. Cabbages and leeks look just as pretty as the petunias!

▲ In the Beaujolais region, the hillsides surrounding each village are covered with vineyards ripening in the sun.

Making the most of the land

Sheep, goats, and cattle are kept in remote areas that are no good for growing crops, such as the Auvergne in the Massif Central. Shepherds drive their flocks to graze on the upland pasture in the summer, and bring them down in winter. This area is famous for cheeses made from cow and sheep milk.

Vineyards

Grapes need deep, well-drained soils and a sunny, frost-free climate. They grow best on south-facing hillsides. The Loire Valley is famous for white and sparkling wines. The best red wine comes from Burgundy in the east, and Bordeaux.

Woods and forests

Trees are important in French cuisine. Almonds, walnuts, and chestnuts are used in cooking, and the leaves are sometimes used to wrap cheeses. In autumn, people gather mushrooms growing under the trees.

FOOD FOR FREE

One of the most expensive vegetables is found by accident! Truffles are fungi, like mushrooms, but they grow underground. They have to be sniffed out by dogs or pigs. One truffle can sell for hundreds of dollars.

Family meals are important. Traditionally, the whole family eats together. But things are changing. People are busy at work and don't always have time to cook.

Starting the day

Breakfast is fresh bread, a croissant or brioche, and coffee with milk. Croissants are made of buttery, flaky pastry. They are eaten with butter and jam. Some people dunk them in the coffee. Brioches are soft, sweet rolls. In the Basque country, near Spain, they drink hot chocolate instead of coffee. French people hardly ever eat cooked food at breakfast.

Lunch or dinner?

Traditionally, the main meal is eaten around 7:30 in the evening. Lunch is a lighter meal eaten at midday. However, some people prefer it the other way round. The main meal consists of at least three courses. It begins with a starter, such as salad, pâté, or soup. This is followed by a main dish of meat or fish with vegetables. Then comes cheese, and finally a dessert or fresh fruit.

▲ A typical French breakfast of coffee, croissant, and jam. These days, younger people often prefer cornflakes and other cereals.

What to drink

Most people drink a glass of wine with lunch and dinner. It doesn't have to be expensive. Supermarkets sell wine in plastic containers for drinking at home. Children are allowed to drink a little wine mixed with water. Most people drink mineral water as well. After the meal, people usually drink a small cup of black coffee.

Teatime treats

Young children have tea, known as *le goûter*, at 4:00 pm when they get home from school. This is usually bread and butter with jam or chocolate spread, and a glass of milk.

BUSY PEOPLE

Shops used to close for two hours at lunchtime, and people went home to eat. These days, they are too busy to stop work for so long. But they like to get out of the office. Most people go to a restaurant for a light lunch, such as an omelette and salad.

▼ Lunch with family and friends tastes even better when it's eaten outdoors.

Eating Out

The French love to eat out. There's so much choice, from restaurants and tiny bistros to cafes. Today there are fast food outlets everywhere, too.

▲ Maxim's, in Paris, is one of the most famous restaurants in the world. Its elegant decoration, in the "art nouveau" style, sets the scene for a very special dinner.

Where to eat?

For a formal meal, people go to a restaurant. Here they may be served up to six courses. There's a fish course before the meat, and sometimes salad is served between courses. Cheese always comes before the dessert.

A celebration meal begins with an alcoholic drink called an aperitif, such as Kir. This is a white wine and blackcurrant cordial. Traditionally, a different wine comes with each course. White wine goes with fish, red wine with meat. There's even a sweet wine to go with the dessert. After all that comes a small glass of brandy to help digestion!

A bistro is a small, informal restaurant serving simpler meals. People usually order only one course and a dessert. They serve typical dishes such as onion soup, pasta, braised meat, and chicken with garlic.

The cafe

At a sidewalk cafe you can order almost anything, at any time of day. People go there for a sandwich or a salad. *Salade niçoise*, with olives, hard-boiled egg, and tuna, is popular. Another delicious light snack is croque-monsieur – a grilled cheese and ham sandwich. They also serve ice cream and cakes.

But you don't have to eat. Some people just order a coffee, then sit and read the paper. They also drink tea, which is considered very "English." A French tisane is a kind of herbal or fruit tea.

▶ Cafes and bistros usually have their special "dish of the day" and fixed-price menu chalked on a blackboard. Once a dish is finished, its name is erased.

French people still prefer to shop daily at the market or in small local shops. They like to buy things fresh every day. There are special shops for each type of food.

Bread and cakes

A French cake shop is called a *pâtisserie*. It sells a huge variety of sponge and pastry cakes, topped with icing or chocolate. Other delicious specialties are meringues, macaroons, chocolate éclairs, and fruit tarts. One, called a *religieuse*, is shaped like a nun!

Next door you might find the bakery– the *boulangerie*. There are lots of different types of bread. The most typical is the long baguette. It has a crisp crust but is soft inside. Baguettes have to be bought fresh every day. They have no preservatives and soon go stale. *Pain de campagne* is a round, country style loaf made from whole-wheat flour.

The cheese shop

France has at least 500 different cheeses! Some, such as Brie and Camembert, are soft and runny inside a white skin. You're supposed to eat the skin, too.

▶ The baker's shop window is full of all kinds of freshly baked bread, rolls, and croissants.

Brie comes from an area southeast of Paris, and Camembert comes from Normandy. Cheeses like these are delicious with a fresh baguette.

Comté is one of the harder cheeses. It comes in a rind, which you *don't* eat. It's usually cut into cubes in a salad or grated on an omelette.

The butcher shop

The *boucherie* sells fresh meat and all kinds of sausages, dried and cured meat, and pâté. Dried and cured meats are called charcuterie. They are often flavored with herbs and spices. You can also see hams and sausages hanging from the ceiling.

▲ This cheese shop, or *fromagerie*, has a tempting display, but these are just a few of France's huge variety of cheeses.

ODD THINGS

In France, no part of an animal is wasted. No one thinks of liver, kidneys, brain, sweetbreads, tripe, or tongue as unpleasant. They are all used in classic dishes in the best restaurants. And, yes, the French really do eat frogs' legs and snails. Cooked in oil and garlic, they're a delicacy!

Food and Religion

There is no state religion in France, but around half the population is Catholic. Even people who no longer go to church regularly are happy to celebrate religious festivals. Most of these involve families getting together and having a good meal.

▲ The festival of St Ronan, held in Locronan, Brittany, is one of the oldest in France. Hundreds of people, some in traditional dress, walk through the countryside carrying banners from the church.

Saints days

There are many saints days in the calendar. Some of these are national holidays; others are just celebrated locally.

The Virgin Mary is a particular favorite in France. The Feast of the Assumption, on August 15, celebrates her entry into heaven. Because it's the middle of summer, people celebrate with picnics and family meals outdoors.

Fish and flesh

Traditionally, Christians were forbidden to eat meat on Fridays. This was in memory of the crucifixion of Jesus, which took place on that day. People ate fish instead. Meat was also forbidden during Lent, the 40-day period leading up to Easter. This is traditionally a period of meditation and penitence.

Today, people are encouraged to give up something they like during Lent, such as chocolate or wine. Strict Catholics still avoid meat on Fridays, and restaurant menus always feature fish dishes on those days.

Easter

Even those who are not religious celebrate Easter as the coming of spring. Eggs are traditionally associated with Easter. On Easter Day, people eat omelettes for breakfast and roast lamb cooked with garlic and rosemary for lunch. Children celebrate with chocolate eggs.

Newcomers

France's growing Muslim population has had an effect on daily life. Many people fast during Ramadan and celebrate the end of this period with the three-day festival of Id-ul-Fitr.

▲ Chocolate Easter eggs, from the world famous company Lenôtre, are decorated by hand.

EASTER BELLS

In French sweet shops you will see chocolate bells alongside Easter eggs. Legend says that before Easter all the church bells in France fly off to Rome to visit the pope. On Easter Day they fly back again, bringing chocolate and gifts for the children.

Happy Christmas!

Christmas in France can last for several weeks. Some children get presents on December 25, while others get theirs earlier, on St Nicholas Day, December 6.

On Christmas Eve, people go to Midnight Mass and then have a late family supper, called the *réveillon*. In Paris, they eat oysters and goose-liver pâté. In Provence, it's roast goose and snails, and in Burgundy they prefer roast turkey.

New Year

Some French people celebrate the New Year more than Christmas. Friends visit each other to exchange gifts of fruit, flowers, and little dishes of sweets and sugared almonds. Traditionally, shopkeepers gave customers little gifts of food.

King for a day

The Feast of the Epiphany, on January 6, celebrates the Three Kings' visit to Jesus. It's a big occasion. People bake a special almond cake called *galette des Rois* (Three Kings' cake). Hidden inside the cake is a toy trinket or charm. Whoever gets the piece of cake with the charm gets to wear a crown as king or queen for the night.

▲ Christmas wouldn't be complete without a *bûche de Noël*, a chocolate cake decorated to look like a log of wood. Traditionally, people used to keep a log burning all through the night on Christmas Eve.

RECIPE: galette des Rois

Equipment
- mixing bowl • spoon • large tart tin • fork • pastry brush

Ingredients
- 2 sheets puff pastry • ⅓ cup (75g) sugar
- ½ cup (100g) ground almonds • 1 egg, beaten
- ¼ cup (50g) softened butter • almond extract
- trinket or charm (that can't melt in the oven!)
- water • 1 egg yolk, beaten

1 Mix the ground almonds, sugar, egg, softened butter, and almond extract in a bowl. Add the trinket or charm (and be sure to watch out for it later!).

2 Press one sheet of pastry into the tart tin and prick with a fork. Spread the mixture onto the pastry.

3 Moisten the edge of the pastry with water. Place the second sheet of pastry on top of the mixture. Press the pastry down with your fingers around the edge to seal it together.

4 Prick the top with a fork a few times (this lets the air out as it cooks). Brush with egg yolk.

5 Cook in a pre-heated oven for 40 minutes at 400°F (200°C).

Feasts and Fireworks

There are lots of other events that the French like to celebrate with parties, fireworks, and food. One of the most important is Bastille Day, on July 14. This celebrates the beginning of the French Revolution.

Mardi Gras

Mardi Gras (Fat Tuesday) is the highlight of the carnival period, which comes before Lent. Traditionally, it was the last chance to have a good time and eat up all the food in the house before fasting began.

The most spectacular celebrations are in Nice, on the south coast. People in fancy dress and masks go out to watch parades of decorated floats and fireworks, and pelt each other with flowers. During carnival, people buy crêpes and other food from street vendors who cook it fresh then and there.

Celebrating the sea

In the coastal region of Brittany they celebrate the local fishing industry with the Fête des Filets Bleus (Festival

◄ The Mardi Gras parade in Nice makes the most of the perfume and colors of the region's flowers.

of the Blue Nets). This is held on the last Sunday in August in the town of Concarneau.

They play traditional music and eat local seafood dishes. You might be served a mixed platter of lobster, crab claws, prawns, oysters, and mussels, fresh from the sea. This is eaten with just a slice of lemon and fresh bread.

Celebrating the seasons

Most rural regions have their own festivals celebrating the harvest of produce or local events. On July 26, the town of Tours in the Loire holds a garlic and basil fair, where local farmers sell their special varieties.

In wine-growing regions, the autumn grape harvest is celebrated with processions, wine tasting, and the election of a harvest queen.

▼ Children in Banyuls-sur-Mer, in the Pyrenees, look forward to the grape harvest festival. They get a chance to stomp the grapes in the traditional way!

The traditional cuisine of the north, where the weather is cool, is hearty. People need good meaty stews to keep them warm.

Brittany

With its dramatic coastline, Brittany is famous for seafood and fish. A favorite dish is *coquille Saint-Jacques* – scallops cooked in white wine and mushrooms and edged with mashed potato and grated cheese. Pancakes are very popular here, too. The savory ones are called galettes, and crêpes are the sweet ones.

Normandy

The very rural area of Normandy is famous for dairy produce and apples, used to make cider. Local dishes mostly feature cream and apples. Meat is cooked in cider and flavored with apple rings and cream. Mussels in cream, garlic, and white wine are another specialty.

▶ The traditional produce of Normandy: apples, cream, butter, and Camembert cheese.

Burgundy and Bordeaux

The best red wine is produced in the southwest and is used generously in cooking. Many of the dishes that we think of as typically French come from here, such as coq au vin and Beef Burgundy. These are chicken and beef cooked in red wine, with mushrooms and other vegetables.

RECIPE: crêpes from Brittany

Equipment
- bowl • sieve • whisk • small frying pan

Ingredients (for 12 crêpes)
- 1 cup (250g) plain flour • pinch of salt
- 2 eggs, beaten • 1 cup (0.25 liter) milk
- 3 tablespoons (40g) melted butter
- a small jar of jam or sugar

1 Sift the flour and salt into a bowl. Make a hollow in the middle and pour in the eggs, milk, and melted butter.

2 Beat well until smooth. Leave to stand for an hour.

3 Ask a grown-up to pour a little of the mixture into a hot, greased frying pan. Cook over a high heat until the underside is golden brown.

4 Turn the crêpe over – or toss it, if you're feeling brave! – and cook the other side. Dust the crêpes with sugar or spread with jam. Roll them up and serve.

The further south you go, the simpler the cooking becomes. People on the south coast of France enjoy a Mediterranean diet – they eat lots of fresh fruit and vegetables, and cook in olive oil.

Provence

If a dish has "provençale" in the title, it means cooked in olive oil with garlic, tomatoes, peppers, and olives. Ratatouille is a famous Provence dish. Another is a fish stew called bouillabaisse. Originally it was made by fishermen's wives from the leftovers their husbands couldn't sell. Now it's a specialty!

The Basque country

The Basque country is a very independent region, with Spanish influences. The food here has strong flavors and is very colorful, with bright red and yellow peppers and tomatoes. A favorite dish is *piperade* – scrambled eggs with red peppers, ham, and tomatoes.

▶ Traditionally, bouillabaisse is served in two dishes. The fish is on one plate, and the "soup" and garlic mayonnaise are in a separate bowl.

RECIPE: ratatouille

Equipment
- cutting board • sharp knife • colander
- paper towels • large saucepan

Ingredients
- 2 eggplants • 3 zucchinis • 2 onions
- 2 red/green peppers, cored, and de-seeded
- 4 tablespoons olive oil
- 2 cloves of garlic, crushed
- 1 tablespoon fresh basil, chopped
- salt and freshly ground black pepper
- 14 oz. (400g) can of Italian tomatoes, well drained, and coarsely chopped

Ask a grown-up to help you with the chopping and hot oil.

1 Chop the eggplants and zucchinis into 1-inch (2.5cm) pieces. Don't chop the pieces too small or they will go mushy. Put them in a colander, sprinkle with salt, and leave to stand for one hour. This stops them from tasting bitter. Dry them on paper towels.

2 Chop the onions coarsely. Chop the peppers into 1-inch (2.5cm) pieces.

3 Heat the oil in a large saucepan and fry the onions and garlic for 10 minutes. Add the peppers, eggplants, zucchinis, and basil. Season with salt and pepper and stir well. Put the lid on and simmer very gently for 30 minutes.

4 Add the tomato and cook for another 15 minutes, with the lid off.

Feeding the World

Because the French are so proud of their own food, it's been hard for other styles of cooking to have much influence in France. But French cuisine has spread all over the world. Chefs learn to cook in France and then open their own restaurants in other countries.

◄ "Tagine" is the name of the stew and also the special cone-shaped pot it is cooked in.

Food from afar

The port of Marseilles is one of France's most cosmopolitan cities. For centuries, people from all over the Mediterranean arrived here with their own food and culture. French people got to know about lots of different types of food. However, it's only recently that chefs have begun to blend unusual foreign ingredients with traditional French recipes.

African influences

The most important influence has been the introduction of food from North Africa. Immigrants began arriving in the 1960s from the former French colonies of Morocco, Algeria, and Tunisia. They brought with them food flavored with spices such as saffron and ginger, and hot harissa paste.

The most typical dish is the Moroccan tagine. This is a stew of meat or chicken and vegetables, flavored with lemon and apricots, nuts and raisins. It is cooked very slowly so the meat is tender, and served with couscous. And a takeout favorite is a kebab and salad in pita bread!

Healthier food

In the 1970s, people began to realize that traditional French dishes, full of butter and cream, were not very healthy. They invented "nouvelle cuisine" – new style cooking. They stopped covering food in rich sauces. Instead, fresh herbs and spices were used for flavoring. They cooked meat for a shorter time and steamed vegetables to keep them crisp.

▶ Nouvelle cuisine is healthy, but sometimes looks more like art than cookery!

THE MICHELIN GUIDE

The famous Michelin restaurant guide was first published in 1900. It helped to introduce people all over the world to French food. Judges award stars to restaurants that serve top-quality cooking – three stars means the chef is a real star.

Glossary

aperitif An alcoholic drink served before the meal to stimulate the appetite.

bistro A small restaurant serving simple meals.

brioche A sweet, buttery bread roll.

chef A professional cook; head of the kitchen.

crêpe A thin pancake, either sweet or savory.

cuisine The style of cooking of a particular country or, literally, "kitchen."

fertile Capable of sustaining healthy growth of plants.

galette (1) A flat, round, crusty cake. (2) A savory pancake made with dark flour.

haute cuisine Cooking in a grand style; literally "high cooking."

hexagon A six-sided shape.

Lent In the Christian calendar, the 40-day period before Easter.

macaroon A sweet made with coconut, almond, and egg white.

marzipan A stiff paste made from ground almonds and sugar, used to make sweets.

Mediterranean (1) The sea, almost completely surrounded by land, which borders Europe, Africa, and Asia. (2) The land areas, particularly of southern Europe, that are closest to the Mediterranean sea.

meringue A crisp cake made from egg white and icing sugar.

omelette A dish made from beaten eggs cooked in butter; served plain or with sweet or savory fillings.

pain de campagne Literally "country bread:" a round loaf made from whole-wheat flour.

pâté Ground meat and/or liver flavored with herbs and pressed into a spreadable paste.

rural Of the countryside.

salade niçoise A salad with vegetables, olives, and tuna.

terrain A piece of ground with particular physical characteristics.

tisane A kind of herbal tea.

truffle A kind of fungus that grows underground.

Further Information

Books

Cooking the French Way by Lynne Marie Waldee (Lerner Publications, 2001)

Flavour of France: Food and Festivals by Teresa Fisher (Wayland, 1998)

I'm the Chef: The Young Chef's French Cookbook by Rosalba Gioffre (Franklin Watts, 2002)

A Taste of Culture: Foods of France by Peggy J Parks (Kidhaven Press, 2005)

Websites

www.circletimekids.com/WorldLibrary/countries/France
Circletime Kids: A website with bilingual resources. It includes simple recipes that children can make.

www.ffcook.com
French Food and Cook: An adult site, but it contains useful information, cookery terms in translation, and recipes.

www.food-links.com/countries/france/french-food-culture.php
Typical French Food: Basic information and links to other sites.

Index